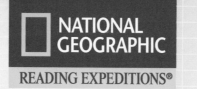

NATIONAL GEOGRAPHIC

READING EXPEDITIONS®

PLANET PATROL

Antarctic Adventure

By Rebecca L. Johnson

Illustrated by Robert Hynes

PICTURE CREDITS
4 (top) © Tom Newsom; 6 (top to bottom)
© Sea World of California/Corbis, Maria Stenzel;
7 Mapping Specialists, Ltd.; 64 (inset) © Charles
Nicklin, (background) © Joan H. Membery,
courtesy Sylvia Earle.

Produced through the worldwide resources of
the National Geographic Society, John M. Fahey,
Jr., President and Chief Executive Officer;
Gilbert M. Grosvenor, Chairman of the Board;
Nina D. Hoffman, Executive Vice President and
President, Books and Education Publishing
Group.

**PREPARED BY NATIONAL GEOGRAPHIC
SCHOOL PUBLISHING**
Ericka Markman, Senior Vice President and
President, Children's Books and Education
Publishing Group; Steve Mico, Senior Vice
President, Publisher, Editorial Director; Francis
Downey, Executive Editor; Richard Easby,
Editorial Manager; Bea Jackson, Director of
Design; Cynthia Olson, Art Director; Margaret
Sidlosky, Director of Illustrations; Matt
Wascavage, Manager of Publishing Services;
Lisa Pergolizzi, Sean Philpotts, Production
Managers, Ted Tucker, Production Specialist.

MANUFACTURING AND QUALITY CONTROL
Christopher A. Liedel, Chief Financial Officer;
Phillip L. Schlosser, Director; Clifton M. Brown,
Manager.

EDITORS
Barbara Seeber, Mary Anne Wengel

BOOK DEVELOPMENT
Morrison BookWorks LLC

BOOK DESIGN
Steven Curtis Design

ART DIRECTION
Dan Banks, Project Design Company

Published by the National Geographic Society
1145 17th Street, N.W.
Washington, D.C. 20036-4688

ISBN-13: 978-0-7922-5852-0

2010 2009 2008
  3 4 5 6 7 8 9 10 11 12 13 14 15

Contents

3

Science on Ice

Dr. Bender took off his glasses and rubbed his tired eyes. He had received many responses from students to the ad he had posted online. He carefully chose the four applications that stood out from the rest. He couldn't wait to let Sam, Jean, Devin, and Sarah know that they'd soon be off to Antarctica!

Sam Davidson
age 11
Sandusky, Ohio
I think birds are great! I watch them through binoculars all the time. Studying birds that "fly" underwater would be fantastic!

Jean Abbott
age 12
Alden, Kansas
I like science, and I like numbers. Recording data and taking pictures are two things I'm good at. I also think they are fun!

4

Attention Young Explorers!

Would you like to study penguins? EcoAware is an organization that is dedicated to promoting science and environmental awareness around the world. EcoAware will give four students, ages 11 to 13, the chance to work with Dr. Thompson in Antarctica for one month. Dr. Thompson is studying the effects of climate change on Adelie penguins. If you are interested, fill out the application below and send it to Dr. Alan Bender at EcoAware.

Devin Weir
age 13
Greeley, Colorado
I want to be an engineer who designs new machines that scientists can use. Someday I'd like to build a robot. Oh, and I like snow, too!

Sarah Huang
age 12
Fife, Washington
Antarctica looks beautiful in the pictures I've seen. But from what I've read, it's also a place where great discoveries are made.

Antarctica

After the interns accepted their assignment, Dr. Bender emailed this fact sheet about Antarctica to them.

ANTARCTICA

Antarctica is a continent. It is mostly covered by thick ice. Very few people live there.

Antarctica is located at the bottom of the world. It is the highest, windiest, and driest continent. Antarctica is very cold. It has the lowest temperatures on Earth.

Scientists from around the world visit Antarctica to study the climate and the animals that live there. This scientist is measuring the depth of snow on an iceberg in Antarctica.

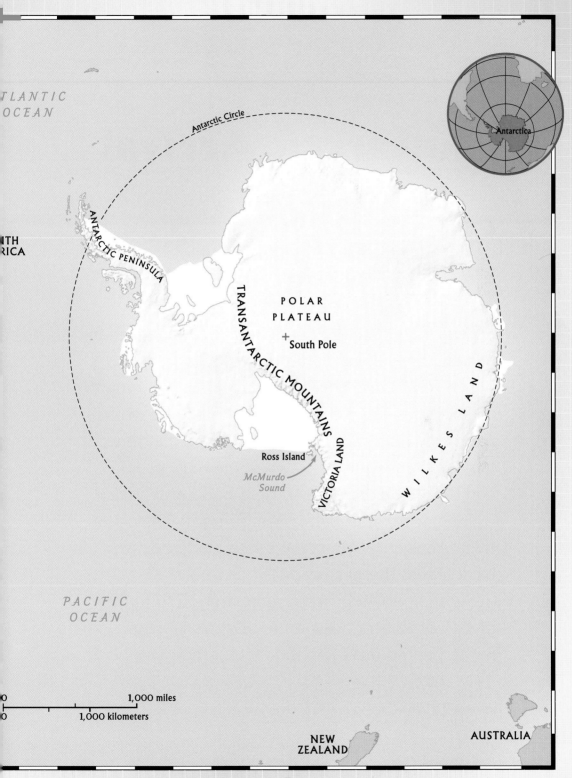

ATLANTIC
OCEAN

Antarctic Circle

SOUTH
AMERICA

ANTARCTIC PENINSULA

POLAR
PLATEAU

+ South Pole

TRANSANTARCTIC MOUNTAINS

VICTORIA LAND

Ross Island

McMurdo
Sound

WILKES LAND

PACIFIC
OCEAN

1,000 miles

1,000 kilometers

NEW
ZEALAND

AUSTRALIA

Antarctica

Antarctic Arrival

Sam peered out the airplane window, amazed by a land of bright white and blue.

"Hey!" he cried above the roar of the plane's engines. "I think I see it!"

Jean unbuckled her seat belt. She squeezed in beside Sam, straining to see.

Directly below the plane was the steely blue ocean. It was flecked all over with dots of white. *Icebergs!* Jean thought as she squinted at the horizon. Sandwiched between the dark ocean and the pale sky was a shining band of white.

Jean grinned at Sam. "You're right! That's got to be Antarctica!" Jean said. She made her way back across the narrow aisle.

Sarah and Devin were soon struggling to their feet. "Let us see!" demanded Devin. He and Sarah peered out the window together.

iceberg - a large floating mass of ice detached from a glacier

Back in her seat, Jean turned to face Dr. Bender. "I can't believe we're really doing this. It's all thanks to you, Dr. Bender. And EcoAware!"

Dr. Bender smiled. "Yes, you're lucky, all of you. Not many people make it to Antarctica. But EcoAware views you as an investment in the world's future. We're hoping this trip will help you become scientists."

"I can't wait to get there!" said Sarah, stepping back from the window. She glanced down the aisle. People were crowded together on either side. They were all dressed like the EcoAware group, in big parkas and rubber boots. Great stacks of boxes filled the back of the plane. Sarah guessed they held food, research equipment, and other supplies.

This wasn't a regular airplane, with comfy seats and an in-flight movie. It was a C-130 cargo plane. The passengers weren't businesspeople or tourists, either. Most of them were scientists. That made Sarah happy. More than anything, she wanted to be a scientist someday, and Antarctica was like a huge outdoor laboratory. No country owned it. But every year, scientists from all over the world came to study it.

Sarah took her seat again. Beside her, Sam was unwrapping an energy bar. He took a big bite.

Sarah glanced at him. Sam always seemed to be eating, but he was very thin. And he was taller than she was. "How many of those have you had?" she asked.

"Four, maybe five," he said, chewing. "It's cold in here. People burn a lot of calories in Antarctica just to keep warm."

"But we haven't even gotten there yet!" Sarah replied with a laugh.

"Speaking of getting there," said Dr. Bender, "have you all finished reading the background materials I gave you?"

"Absolutely!" said Devin. He sat up straight, as if he were going to give a lecture. "As interns with the international organization EcoAware," he began, "our assignment is to work with Dr. Ben Thompson. Dr. Thompson is an expert on Adélie penguins." Devin pointed a finger at Sam. "Sam! Tell us about Adélies!"

"Ahhhemmm!" said Sam, clearing his throat. "Adélie penguins are one of 17 different species of penguins in the world. Adélies live along the coast of Antarctica and its islands. They stand about 30 inches tall and weigh roughly 11 pounds. For those using the metric system, that's 76 centimeters and about 5 kilograms."

Dr. Bender chuckled.

"And now, Sarah," said Devin, turning to her. "What do Adélies eat?"

"Some fish, but mostly krill!" Sarah answered quickly, her brown eyes sparkling. "Krill are small, shrimplike animals. They are really important in the Antarctic food web. Some whales and seals eat krill, too."

Jean picked up the story: "Krill feed on algae. Those are tiny plantlike cells. A lot of algae get trapped in sea ice when it forms on the ocean around Antarctica every winter. When the ice melts in the spring, the algae are released. Algae are food for krill. And krill are food for penguins and other ocean animals."

"And right now," Devin went on, "krill populations seem to be changing down here at the bottom of the world. Scientists think that

global warming—that's the steady warming of the planet—is reducing the sea ice that forms each winter. Less sea ice means less trapped algae. And less algae means fewer krill."

"Our job," said Sam, "is to help Dr. Thompson. It's summer now in Antarctica. Penguins are nesting along the coast. Dr. Thompson is using Adélie penguins to find out if krill numbers are up or down in this part of Antarctica."

"If krill numbers are down," Jean concluded, suddenly serious, "that could be bad for penguins and other krill-eating Antarctic animals. That's what we'll try to find out!"

Dr. Bender looked pleased. "I guess I picked the right people for the job." He paused. "Don't forget to write in your journals every day. Your notes will come in handy when you write your final report to EcoAware."

"I've already started mine," Jean said proudly. She pulled out her journal. The first page was full of facts about Antarctica.

Devin had turned to stare out the window again. "Wow! I can see the ice edge!"

global warming - the steady warming of the planet, which causes changes in the climate

Antarctica Notes   by Jean
- The continent of Antarctica covers about 5,400,000 square miles.
- Antarctica is the coldest, driest, and windiest place on Earth.
- Most of the Antarctic continent is covered in snow and ice. The ice is several miles thick in some places.
- Although it snows quite a lot along Antarctica's coast, very little snow falls in the interior. It's actually drier there than in the Sahara Desert.
- The lowest temperature ever recorded in Antarctica was −128.6 degrees Fahrenheit (-89.2 degrees Celsius) at Vostok Station, several hundred miles from the South Pole.
- Most of the people who visit Antarctica each year are scientists.

Iceberg

Jean and Sarah each took another turn at the window. The ice edge was where the open ocean met the sea ice around the continent. Beyond the sea ice was Antarctica itself. The only parts of the landscape not buried in ice and snow were the jagged peaks of tall mountains.

Finally it was Sam's turn at the window. "Hey! We're passing over the coast," he said excitedly. "Somewhere down there are the penguins we're going to study."

Suddenly the sound of the engines changed. The interns could feel the shift as the plane's nose angled down. Sarah noticed some passengers putting on their hats and mittens. She tugged at Sam's sleeve, pulling him away from the window. "Everybody's gearing up," she said. "I'll bet the plane is about to land."

Sarah zipped up her parka and pulled on her mittens. Sam snugged up the laces on his boots. Jean tugged a fleece hat down over her curly brown hair. Devin zipped up his parka and pulled up the hood.

Above the sound of the engines came a low rumbling noise. "Must be the landing gear!" Devin shouted over the noise. Minutes later, the plane touched down. It gradually slowed and then stopped. A door opened near the front. A bright white light flooded in.

"Put on your sunglasses," Jean reminded everyone. "It's bright out there." They all stepped out of the plane into a frozen white world.

Survival School

The cold was so strong when Jean stepped off the plane that her face burned and her eyes watered. She felt her tears freeze on her eyelashes.

A bearded man in a big parka stepped up to the group. It was so cold, the snow squeaked beneath his boots. "Welcome to Antarctica! You must be from EcoAware. I'm Dr. Ben Thompson."

"Alan Bender, director of EcoAware," Dr. Bender said, extending his hand. "And these are the four interns we've arranged to work with you for the next few weeks."

"Pleased to meet you," said Dr. Thompson. He shook all of their mittened hands as they introduced themselves. "Just call me Doc."

They all climbed aboard a big truck with huge tires. Ten minutes later they were at the research station. The scientists working there often traveled out into the wilds of Antarctica to study its glaciers, volcanoes, geology, and wildlife.

Doc showed the interns to their rooms. Then he led them on a tour of the station. They saw the storage area for food and fuel, the machine shop, the medical center, and the helicopter landing pad. They ended up at the science lab where Doc had his small office.

Pictures of penguins covered the office walls. "Did you take these, Doc?" Jean asked. She felt in her pocket for the digital camera she always carried. Documenting their experience with pictures was her job.

"Yes, I did, Jean. I took them at the penguin **rookery** at Cape Bird," Doc replied. "That's where my study site is and where we'll be working. It's 20 kilometers—or about 12 miles—from the station. Let me show you."

The interns crowded around as Doc spread out a map. He pointed out the station and then he pointed to the penguin rookery. "And that," he said, with his finger on a tiny dot, "is the hut where we'll be living for the next month."

Without warning, Sam's stomach growled.

Doc and Dr. Bender both laughed. "I'd say it's time for dinner!" Doc said. "Grab your parkas, everyone." It was a quick walk through the snow to the research station's cafeteria.

"The day after tomorrow—if the weather allows—we'll fly out to the penguin rookery," Doc explained as they ate.

"I can't wait to get out there and meet the penguins!" Sam exclaimed between bites. "Why can't we go tomorrow, Doc?"

"Survival school first. Then penguins," said Dr. Bender.

---

rookery - the nests or breeding place of a penguin colony

Sarah stopped eating. "Why do we need to go to survival school?" she asked. "We'll be with Doc at the rookery. He's an Antarctic expert."

Doc's eyes crinkled up at the corners as he laughed. "Well, thanks for the compliment, Sarah! But everyone who does field work goes through survival school first. That's the rule. Antarctica can be a very dangerous place. The weather here can change amazingly fast. You need to be prepared . . . for anything, at any time."

Early the next day, Sam, Devin, Jean, and Sarah said goodbye to Dr. Bender. He told them that he'd return at the end of the month, when they were done with their assignment.

An hour later, the four interns were on a flat, snowy plain two miles from the station. Devin pulled out the pocket thermometer he'd been given at the lab. Did the thermometer really read -8 degrees Fahrenheit?

"Minus eight, eh?" said Robert, their survival school instructor. "Pretty typical for a summer day here along Antarctica's coast. If you're cold, though, don't worry. I'll have you warmed up soon enough."

First, Robert taught them how to drive safely on snowmobiles. They practiced on a course marked with flags. After that, he had them gather around a big, orange duffel bag.

"Remember to always carry this survival gear when you're traveling," Robert said, holding up the bag. "High winds can spring up in seconds here. Add a little blowing snow and you've got an instant blizzard."

"How long do blizzards last?" Jean asked.

"It depends," Robert replied. "Sometimes a few hours. Sometimes several days."

Sam whistled softly.

Robert continued as he unzipped the duffle bag. "In here you've got a tent, sleeping bags, a small stove, and some emergency food." He winked at them. "All the comforts of home!"

First, Robert showed them how to set up the tent. Next, they practiced starting the stove. They learned how melt snow for water.

"Now let's imagine your tent blew away," said Robert. "How do you stay warm? You build a shelter using snow."

Robert spent the next few hours showing them how to build snow mounds. First, they made two big piles of gear. Then they shoveled snow over the gear to make two large, rounded mounds. With their shovels, they packed the snow down hard. Outside each mound, they dug a small tunnel that started at the edge of the mound and came up just under the piled-up gear. They pulled the gear out through the tunnel. They ended up with two hollowed-out mounds, each large enough to hold two people.

By the time the snow mounds were done, the interns were tired. For an energy boost, they ate chocolate bars. Sam smiled when Robert told them that eating chocolate was also a very good way to keep warm. His smile got even bigger when Robert said they could eat all the chocolate they wanted!

"OK, everyone," Robert said, after he'd looked over their work. "It's time for your final exam."

"There's a test?" asked Jean nervously. "I didn't know we were supposed be studying for a test."

"You've been studying all day," replied Robert. "Your test is that you have to stay overnight in your shelters."

Sarah stared at him, wide-eyed. "Please tell me you're kidding. Stay out here, overnight?"

"Yup!" said Robert. He handed them each a small bag. "For dinner, just add hot water to these freeze-dried meals. Then get some sleep. I'll be over there," he said, pointing to a tent nearby, "in case you need anything. You will be leaving early in the morning for the rookery."

The hot food tasted wonderful. As they were cleaning up, Jean glanced at her watch.

"Wow! It's nearly 11 p.m.!" she exclaimed, looking up at the bright sky. "Summer in Antarctica is pretty strange. Not only is it cold, but the sun never sets!"

"I know," Sarah agreed. "The sunlight kept me awake last night. I wrote about it in my journal." She yawned suddenly. "But nothing will keep me awake tonight." She looked over at the boys' snow mound. They were already inside.

> Antarctic Seasons
>
> by Sarah
>
> Because Antarctica is in the Southern Hemisphere, the seasons are the opposite of what they are in the Northern Hemisphere. When it is winter in the United States, it's summer in Antarctica and vice versa. Antarctica's position at the pole also means that the sun doesn't set during the summer. And during the winter, it never rises. In a sense, the Antarctic summer is one long day, while the Antarctic winter is one long night.

Jean and Sarah crawled through the narrow entrance and into their snow mound. A soft, blue light filtered through the roof of snow over their heads.

"This is fun," said Jean, snuggling deep into her sleeping bag.

"Yeah, it is," admitted Sarah. "But I can't imagine that we're ever going to use all these survival skills. Can you?"

Jean didn't answer. She was already asleep.

Fifty Thousand Penguins

Whoop-whoop-whoop. The blades of the helicopter spun faster and faster. Devin watched the pilot flip switches and check gauges. Seconds later, they were airborne.

The helicopter flew along the coastline and over the sea ice. The ice was solid during the winter. Now that it was summer, it was melting and breaking up into big chunks called **floes.**

"What are those dark blobs down there on that floe?" Sarah asked, pointing out her window.

"Those are Weddell seals," replied Doc. "They spend a lot of time in the water, hunting for fish. But they come up onto the ice to rest."

Ten minutes later, the helicopter gently touched down on a pebbly, snow-streaked beach. Grabbing their gear, Doc and the

floe - a floating piece of ice formed in a large sheet on the surface of a body of water

interns jumped out. Then, with a rush of air, the helicopter was gone. Suddenly it was very quiet.

Steep cliffs rose up on one side of the beach. On the other side was the ocean. It was dotted with big floes. Farther out, several enormous icebergs glinted in the sun.

"Where are the penguins?" Sam asked.

Doc smiled. "Follow me." He set off down the beach, toward a steep ridge. It was a harder climb than it looked. Huffing and puffing, they finally reached the top.

For a moment, the interns just stared. Stretched out in front of them was a beach jam-packed with penguins. And all the penguins seemed to be

talking at once. The sound of their strange, chattering calls filled the air.

"How many penguins are there?" asked Sam.

"About fifty thousand," Doc replied.

Jean pulled out her camera and started taking pictures. Many penguins were sitting on nests. Others were walking to and from the ocean to eat or swim. It was hard not to laugh at the way the penguins walked. With every step, their plump, black-and-white bodies swayed back and forth.

A puff of wind swept up ridge. A sour, musty odor washed over them. "What's that smell?" asked Sarah, wrinkling up her nose.

"Ah, that's the wonderful scent of a penguin rookery, Sarah," Doc said, with a laugh. "Adélies have been nesting here for hundreds of years. Their droppings collect over time. When the ground thaws a bit in the summer, the odor can get pretty strong."

Doc pointed out a small, square building above the rookery. Three snowmobiles were parked beside it. "That's the hut I showed you on the map. It's going to be our base camp for studying the penguins," he explained. "We'll drop off our gear there and have some lunch."

The hut had one big room for cooking and working, and two small rooms with bunk beds. Doc started the heater. In minutes, the hut was toasty warm. While the interns unpacked, he made grilled cheese sandwiches.

After they had eaten lunch, Doc spread out a map of the rookery on the table. "Here's where we are and here's the study site," he said, tapping the map with his finger. "To get there, we'll walk right through the rookery, so watch your step. The nests are very close together."

Minutes later, the interns followed Doc, single file, as he led the way. Jean thought the penguins would be afraid of them. But most were just curious. They stared back at Jean with shiny black, white-rimmed eyes. Some penguins paid no attention at all. They were too busy feeding their fluffy chicks or rearranging the stones that made up their nests.

"Here we are," said Doc as they walked up to a group of nests. A knee-high mesh fence went around the nests. It formed a sort of corral. The fence was too high for the penguins to jump. To get in or out of the corral, the penguins had to walk across a small bridge set into the fence.

"There are 12 nests inside the corral," Doc explained, crouching down by the fence. "With two birds to a nest, that means there are 24 adult penguins in our study."

"Why study only 24?" Devin asked.

"Well, the penguins inside the corral form what scientists call a representative sample," Doc replied. "It would be physically impossible to study all 50,000 penguins in the rookery. So we study a small group. We assume that what the members of that group do is pretty much what all the other penguins in the rookery are doing, too."

Doc stood up. "As you know, the idea behind my research project is to use penguins to find out how abundant krill are in the ocean. Are there as many krill as in past years? Or are there fewer now that global temperatures are going up?"

Doc walked over to the bridge. "This bridge is really a scale in disguise. Parent penguins take turns going to sea to catch food for their chicks. Every time a penguin crosses the bridge, it gets weighed. So we know how much it weighs when it goes out and comes back."

A look of understanding suddenly spread across Jean's face. "And the difference between those two weights," she said excitedly, "is a measure of how much food they have in their stomachs."

"Exactly!" said Doc.

"But how do you keep track of which penguin is which?" Devin asked.

"The same way we keep track of them when they're out at sea, Devin," Doc answered with a smile. "Every adult penguin inside the corral is wearing a radio transmitter."

"Oh, so that's what those things are on their backs! They look like a pack of cards with a tail," said Devin, pointing at a penguin in the corral.

Doc smiled. "Yes. The 'tail' is the antenna. The transmitters also contain a tiny, electronic ID chip. When a penguin crosses the bridge, a scanner records the ID number at the same time the scale records the weight."

As if on cue, a penguin inside the corral came waddling across the bridge. It passed in front of the sensor. The interns heard a faint beep as the information was recorded.

"When the penguins are out at sea, we track their exact location with a receiver like this," said Doc. He pulled a small device out of his parka pocket and held it up.

"At the end of every day," he went on, "we'll use the data from the receivers to make maps showing where each penguin went on its feeding trips. From the bridge data, we can calculate how much food each penguin was carrying on its return. When we combine the maps and the weights, we can estimate how much krill the penguins are finding in the ocean and how far they have to travel to get it."

"It's kind of like figuring out where the grocery store is, isn't it?" asked Sarah. "And if the shelves are stocked." Everyone laughed.

Doc glanced at his watch. "Tomorrow, you'll start observing the penguins and helping me to collect data," he said. "But there's one more thing I want to show you today. Sometimes when a penguin is far out at sea, you can't pick up its transmitter signal from here. If that happens, we'll try from that ridge." He pointed.

The interns all looked to the area where Doc was pointing. "That's a very long walk," Jean said.

"Fortunately, there's a shortcut," Doc told Jean. "We can get there by snowmobile. Come on, I'll show you guys."

Back at the hut, Doc grabbed several pairs of binoculars. They loaded survival bags on the snowmobiles. With Doc in the lead, they drove on a snowy path that ran along the top of the rookery. The path was marked with bamboo poles topped with small, colored flags.

The flagged path ended on the far side of the rookery. "This is the place," explained Doc, as they walked along the ridge. "The reception is usually better up here."

"And there's a fantastic view," said Sarah. She gazed out over the rookery and the ocean. "Hey, look at those penguins!"

Not far from shore, a group of penguins dove off a small iceberg into the water.

"Brrrr!" exclaimed Jean. "I can't imagine going swimming in that icy cold water."

"That's the beauty of blubber," Doc remarked. "Like seals and whales, penguins have a thick layer of that special fat. Blubber keeps their body heat in and the cold out."

The Antarctic Treaty   by Sarah

In 1959, 12 nations signed the first
Antarctic Treaty. The treaty makes it
illegal for anyone to hunt, hurt, or bother
the wildlife. Only scientists with special
permits can touch penguins or other wild
animals. Scientists can only touch the animals

Transmitter

to weigh or measure them, or to attach research instruments
to their bodies. These instruments must be designed to fall off
on their own. Or they must be easy to take off.

Sam had been watching the penguins through the binoculars. "Hey," he said suddenly. "There's a seal out there."

Doc and the interns grabbed their binoculars. They all spotted the dark head in the water.

"It's a leopard seal," Doc said.

"Do leopard seals eat fish, like Weddell seals?" Sarah asked.

"No, Sarah. They eat penguins," Doc replied.

Through binoculars, they saw the seal swim toward a big floe where several penguins stood.

Without warning, the seal slipped beneath the water's surface.

"Oh no! It's gone," lamented Devin.

"Not necessarily," said Doc. "Keep your eye on those penguins."

A minute passed. Then two. Then suddenly the leopard seal came exploding out of the water, right at the edge of the floe. It grabbed one of the penguins closest to the edge in its huge jaws. Seal and penguin vanished below the surface.

"Oh, no!" wailed Sarah. "The poor penguin!"

"I understand how you feel, Sarah," Doc said sympathetically. "But the seal has to eat, too. So do its pups. Leopard seals are predators, and their prey are penguins."

Sarah knew that Doc was right. But she still felt sorry for the penguin.

Doc tucked his binoculars inside of his parka. "OK, gang. Let's head back to the hut. Tomorrow your work begins."

They climbed onto the snowmobiles and drove back along the flagged route. The sun cast an orange glow on the rookery and the icebergs.

Antarctica's Wildlife   by Devin

Most of Antarctica's wildlife lives in the ocean. The cold water is full of fish, whales, seals, and penguins. Tonight Sam spotted a leopard seal in the water. It looked very different from the Weddell seal we saw on the flight out. It caught a penguin while we watched. Doc says leopard seals hide under floes and small icebergs. Any penguins standing at the edge of the ice are in danger of being caught by the seals.

In the Rookery

"Day six," Sarah said softly to herself as she walked down to the study site.

They had done a lot in six days. Jean had taken hundreds of pictures. Sam had made dozens of sketches. All four interns had spent hours sitting by the corral, watching the penguins and taking detailed notes about what they were doing.

When the penguins weren't sleeping, they were always busy. They cleaned their feathers. They fed their chicks. They snatched stones from their neighbors' nests. Each time a penguin returned from a trip to the ocean, it did a little dance with its mate. The two birds faced each other, swaying back and forth. Then they threw back their heads and let loose with a raspy, rattling call.

With Doc's help, the interns had quickly learned how to use the receivers and track the penguins at sea. At the end of every day, they downloaded data from the bridge and the receivers. Then they hiked up to the hut. After dinner, they sat around Doc's computer and analyzed all the information they'd gathered. They made charts of how much food the penguins had brought back to their nests that day. They also made maps showing where the penguins were finding krill out at sea. Everything had worked perfectly.

Adélie penguins   by Sam
- Adélies spend winters at sea hunting for food in the water and resting on icebergs.
- In the spring, tens of thousands of Adélies gather at nesting grounds called rookeries.
- Adélie penguins build nests of small stones.
- Female Adélies typically lay two greenish-white eggs in early November. The eggs hatch in about a month. The chicks have a thick coat of gray down feathers.
- The parent penguins go out to sea to catch food for their chicks. In three weeks, the chicks are almost full-grown.
- When the chicks grow black-and-white feathers, they can swim and feed on their own.

For six days, the weather had been perfect, too. But today, a gusty, bitter-cold wind whipped through the rookery. Sarah pulled up the hood of her parka.

"Hey, Sarah!" called Sam as she walked up. "Where's Doc?"

"He's still up at the hut," Sarah answered. "He wanted to finish writing up a report."

Just then, a penguin returning from the ocean stepped up onto the bridge. Sam eyed the scanner. As it beeped, the penguin's ID number flashed on the screen.

"Number 4!" cried Sam. He blew on his fingers to warm them. Then he wrote the penguin's number and return time in his notebook. "Number 4 chicks—get ready for dinner!"

Number 4 waddled up to its nest. His mate, Number 3, got up from the nest. Two fluffy chicks instantly started begging for food. Number 4

bent down and opened his mouth. Krill plopped out onto the ground. The chicks pecked at them hungrily.

"Hungry, Sarah?" Sam teased, as he started writing a description of the chicks' begging behavior. "Those krill still look fresh."

Jean and Devin were crouched on the other side of the corral, trying to get out of the wind. They were watching penguin Number 17. They'd nicknamed him Growler because of the strange sounds he made.

They'd given names to other penguins, too. Number 3 was Satin because her feathers were so shiny. They called Number 5 Big Eye. He could open his white-rimmed eyes wider than any other penguin they'd seen.

The interns knew they shouldn't get attached to any of the penguins. But they did have a favorite. Number 7 was the smallest penguin in the group. He was very curious. Once they found him peeking into Jean's backpack, nudging it with his beak. Sometimes he watched them while they were writing in their notebooks.

As Jean and Devin watched Growler, Number 7 got off his nest and headed for the bridge. As he passed Growler's nest, the growling bird stabbed out with his beak. But little Number 7 sidestepped the jab neatly and hurried off.

"That was lucky," said Devin to Jean. He knew how painful a poke from a penguin's beak could be. "Hey, that's it!" he said to Sarah and Sam. "Let's call Number 7 'Lucky,' OK?"

They all agreed that the name seemed to fit.

Just then they heard a shout above the wind. "Here comes Doc!" said Jean. She waved to the scientist as he approached. Doc was smiling, as usual. But in the next instant, Doc suddenly slipped and fell.

Devin was the first to reach him. "Doc, are you OK?" he asked, taking Doc by the arm.

"Slipped on that ice," Doc muttered as he sat up. "Aaarrhh!" he cried out, wincing in pain. "I think I've sprained my ankle."

"Hang on, Doc," said Sam, grabbing Doc's other arm. "We'll get you back to the hut."

With all four interns helping, Doc hobbled back up to the hut. He took off his boots. The sprained ankle had already started to swell.

"Well, it looks like I'm out of commission for a day or two," Doc said grimly.

Sarah started making everyone something hot to eat. "Don't worry, Doc," she said, opening a big can of soup. "We can handle things at the study site."

After they'd eaten, Jean sat down in front of the computer. She started pulling together the data they'd gathered that day.

"By the way," said Doc as he put a cold pack on his ankle, "I compared our results so far with the results I got here last year."

"Are the penguins finding fewer krill this year?" Sam asked anxiously.

"So far, our penguins seem to be coming back with full stomachs," Doc replied. "The krill around Cape Bird appear to be as abundant as they were last year."

Sam let out a sigh of relief.

Doc continued. "But—I got an e-mail today from a penguin scientist working on the Antarctic peninsula. The penguins there are having trouble finding krill."

"Is it warmer up there?" Sarah asked, listening to the wind howl outside the hut.

Doc nodded. "Yes. Temperatures around the peninsula are much warmer than they were just a few years ago. It looks as if global warming is affecting the sea ice there. It's causing the ice to melt earlier in the spring. And as you know, that means fewer algae. That means there are fewer krill for the penguins to eat."

"That's confusing," commented Devin. "Why wouldn't the results be the same everywhere around Antarctica?"

"Well, Devin, this is a big continent," Doc replied. "Conditions aren't exactly the same from place to place. It's possible that global warming will change conditions differently in different places, at least for a while. Figuring out what's going on is a tricky task."

Effects of Temperature   by Devin

Over the past 50 years, there has been a noticeable increase in Antarctica's average temperature. This warming has caused sea ice to decline a lot. Less sea ice means fewer algae, and therefore, fewer krill.

Since the mid-1990s, Adélie penguin populations along the Antarctic Peninsula have fallen by roughly 50 percent as the krill population has declined. Farther south, however, there's actually been a slight increase in the number of Adélies—at least for now.

Doc shifted the cold pack on his ankle, and went on. "The best we can do is gather data and make observations. We hope that what we discover will eventually give us a clear answer as to what the effects of global warming are on algae, krill, and Adélie penguins."

While Doc had been talking, Jean had been quietly staring at the computer screen. She frowned. She jumped up and pulled her notebook out of her backpack. She flipped to one page and studied it. Then she looked at the computer screen again. Her frown got deeper.

Doc noticed the look on her face. "What's the matter, Jean?" he asked.

"We have a problem," she said quietly. "One of our penguins is missing."

The other interns gathered around her.

"Look," Jean said, pointing to the computer screen. "These are data from the weigh bridge. Penguin Number 7, Lucky, crossed the bridge and headed out to sea at 2:18 p.m. He's usually gone for about an hour. But according to these readings, he still hadn't returned at 6:30 p.m. That was the last time I downloaded data, Doc, just before you got hurt."

Jean pushed a key on the keyboard. "Now here's a map I just made using Lucky's transmitter data. We picked up his location offshore here, here, and here," she said, pointing at the map on the screen. "But there are no data points that show him coming back to shore. In other words,

we stopped picking up his signal." She paused.
"Or something stopped it."

For a moment, no one spoke.

Sam put their fears into words. "Do you
suppose," he said haltingly, "that Lucky was
eaten by the leopard seal?"

The question seemed to echo through the hut.

Whiteout!

"Wait a minute!" Sarah protested. "Don't jump to conclusions. Lucky might have returned to the study site after we left."

"What about losing the signal?" Jean asked.

"Well, maybe his transmitter failed," Sarah responded. "It's possible, right, Doc?"

"Any piece of equipment can fail," Doc admitted. "Sarah's right. We don't have any real evidence yet to say what might have happened to Lucky."

"Then let's get some," Devin said firmly. "We should go down to the study site right now to make sure he's not there."

"I should come with you," said Doc, starting to get up. A look of pain showed on his face.

"No way, Doc," said Sam. "We can do this. We'll take a radio so we can stay in touch."

Minutes later, when the interns walked out the door, the wind seemed even stronger. It wasn't long before they were back at the corral. They scanned the nests inside the corral. Lucky was not there.

"Let's see if he crossed the bridge," said Jean. "He might have returned while we were gone, and then gone out to sea again." She pressed a button and a display lit up. Number 11 and Number 3 had crossed since they'd gone back to the hut, but not Number 7.

"I'll see if I can pick up his signal," Sarah said. She pulled a receiver out of her parka pocket and turned it on. She stood completely still, listening for a full minute. "Nothing," Sarah said in a discouraged voice.

Devin had been very quiet. Now he suddenly spoke up. "Maybe Lucky is far out at sea. Maybe we just can't pick up his signal from down here on the beach."

"The ridge!" cried Sarah. "We need to try to get a signal on the ridge!"

Sam pressed a button on the radio he took along with him from the hut. He spoke into it. "Doc, are you there? Doc?"

Doc's voice came booming out. "Of course. Tell me what's happening."

Sam filled him in and then asked about the trip to the ridge. For a moment the radio was silent. Then Doc came back on. "OK. But we need two teams. If Lucky comes back to the study site, someone should be there."

"Doc's right," Sam said. "Sarah, you're the receiver expert. And you're the best snowmobile driver, Devin. You two drive out to the ridge. Jean and I will stay here."

Sarah and Devin hurried back to the hut. "I should go with you," said Doc. "But with this ankle, I'll just slow you down. Besides, the trip to the ridge and back shouldn't take you more than 30 minutes. We'll all stay in touch by radio."

Sarah moved quickly. She stuffed a backpack with food, water, and warm clothes. Outside, Devin started the snowmobile. After a few sputters, it roared to life.

"Don't forget the survival gear!" Doc shouted, as Sarah started out the door.

"We're only going across to the ridge. I can see it from here!" Sarah protested.

"Sarah, take the bag!" Doc said firmly.

"Oh, all right," said Sarah, shaking her head. She grabbed the big, orange duffel bag. Outside, she heaved it onto the back of the snowmobile and strapped it into place. Then she hopped on behind Devin. "Let's go!" she shouted.

The flags on the bamboo poles were whipping back and forth. Devin crouched low behind the windshield, trying to stay out of the wind.

At the ridge, the wind seemed even stronger. As soon as Devin stopped the snowmobile, Sarah leaped off. She pulled two receivers out of her backpack. She flicked on the radio.

"Doc, we're here! We're at the ridge," Sarah said into the radio.

"Great!" Doc replied. "Keep me posted."

Sarah thrust one of the receivers into Devin's hand. "Here, you try, too!" They turned the receivers to Lucky's transmitter frequency. They listened breathlessly, straining to hear. But the only sound they heard was the wind.

"Look!" said Devin, pointing back toward the rookery. "Can you see Sam and Jean, down by the corral?" he asked.

"Yes," Sarah said as she squinted into the wind. She could just make out two parkas.

Then Sarah looked past the rookery. For the first time she noticed the dark gray bank of clouds on the southern horizon. It seemed to grow as she watched, spreading out across the sky.

"Devin," she said pointing. "What's that?"

Devin stared at the band of clouds. "I'd guess it's a storm," he said grimly. "And it's moving fast."

"Let's climb those rocks over there," Sarah said. "Being higher might help."

Devin hesitated. "OK," he agreed. "One more try. But then we head back."

Sarah nodded and strode out toward the rocks. The wind tugged at their clothes. The ocean below was now flecked with whitecaps.

On top of the rocks, Sarah held the receiver up to her ear. "I think I hear something!" she cried.

Devin listened closely to the device in his hand. After a few seconds, he shook his head. "All I hear is static."

"I'm sure there was a beep!" she said. "Maybe if we climb higher …"

Suddenly, a shadow fell over them.

Devin and Sarah both looked up. What had been a dark bank of clouds on the horizon was now a dark dome directly overhead. Devin glanced down at the rookery. It was vanishing behind a white curtain of blowing snow.

Devin grabbed Sarah's arm. "Come on! We're leaving! NOW!"

They quickly scrambled down the rocks. They leaned into the wind, making their way to the snowmobile. Devin started to hop on. But as he looked down the flagged path, he could only see the first two flags. Beyond that was a white blur.

"We have to stop! It's a blizzard! We can't travel in this!" Devin shouted, unhooking the survival bag. He pulled Sarah down beside the snowmobile. "Let's set up the tent right here. The snowmobile will form a windbreak!"

Sarah nodded as she tugged open the bag.

The wind howled. Blowing snow stung their faces. But in minutes, the tent was up. Devin shoved the survival bag into the tent's open door. Sarah crawled inside, with Devin right behind her. He quickly zipped the door shut.

For a few seconds they knelt on the tent floor, panting. "Sleeping bags!" said Sarah, shivering. She pulled two sleeping bags out of the survival kit. They took off their boots and snowy parkas and each crawled into a bag.

Outside, the wind was so strong it sounded as if someone were screaming.

"Sarah, where's the radio?"

Sarah dug the radio out of her parka pocket. Devin pushed the transmit button. "Doc, this is Devin," he said into the radio. "Do you read me?"

A burst of static. Then Doc's voice. "Devin! We were beginning to worry. That storm came up surprisingly fast. What's happening up there?"

"We're fine," Devin replied. "We decided not to drive back in storm. We're still on the ridge, inside the survival tent."

Sam's voice came over the radio. "Do you have enough food and water?"

Devin had to laugh. "Don't worry, Sam! We've got enough food to last for days!"

Doc came back on: "We're all safe here. I radioed the station. This storm is moving really fast. So just stay put. And leave your radio on. I'll be calling you every 30 minutes!"

"Roger, Doc," Devin said. "We'll stay right here. Devin and Sarah out."

Devin put the radio where he could easily reach it. "You know," he said, zipping up his bag, "it's really not all that bad in here."

"You're right," agreed Sarah. "But it sounds terrible outside." The blowing snow made a

hissing sound as it struck the tent. "I guess
Robert and Doc were right about the weather,"
she admitted.

"How do you think the penguins will survive
this storm?" Devin asked.

"I don't know," Sarah answered. She thought
about the penguins and their chicks and sighed.
"I guess we'll find out."

Lost and Found

Sarah checked her watch. Three hours and twenty minutes had passed since the blizzard started. Doc was due to call again in ten minutes.

Devin was reading an old comic book. He'd found it at the bottom of the survival bag. He stopped reading and looked up.

"Hey, Sarah," he said. "Listen."

Sarah listened for a moment. "To what? I don't hear anything."

"That's what I mean," Devin replied. "I think the wind stopped." He unzipped the tent door.

Moments later, Sarah and Devin were standing beside the tent. The blizzard was over. The sky was clearing. In a few minutes, the sun would be out.

All around them, everything was covered with snow. Sarah pulled out her binoculars. She scanned the rookery.

"Are the penguins OK?" Devin asked anxiously.

Sarah smiled and handed him the binoculars. "We didn't have anything to worry about. Look!"

Through the binoculars Devin saw that the penguins were doing what they'd always done. Many were heading for the ocean. A few were sliding down snowy slopes on their tummies!

"It doesn't look as if the snow bothered them at all!" Devin exclaimed. "I guess penguins are a lot better adapted to the cold than we are."

From inside the tent, the radio crackled and they heard Doc's voice. "Sarah? Devin? Come in!"

Sarah reached into the tent for the radio. "We're here, Doc!"

"The storm's over. We're getting ready to come and get you," Doc explained.

"Don't bother, Doc," Sarah replied. "It's clear here, too. We're on our way back. We should be there in fifteen minutes."

It didn't take long to take down the tent and repack the survival bag. Devin slung it up onto the snowmobile. He turned to Sarah.

"All set?"

"Just about," she said quietly. "I want to try to locate Lucky one more time." She pulled the receiver out of her pocket.

"Sarah . . . I don't think . . . " Devin began, shaking his head.

Sarah cut him off. "I know. But I'm still going to try." She turned on the receiver and held it out toward the ocean.

The receiver didn't beep. There was no signal from Lucky.

Sarah turned the receiver off and tucked it back into her pocket. Devin saw tears in her eyes. "OK. Let's go," she said sadly, striding toward the snowmobile.

Ten minutes later, Devin and Sarah pulled up beside the hut.

Jean came running out. "Boy, are we glad to see you!" She gave them each a big hug.

Sam poked his head out the door. "Do you want butter or maple syrup with your pancakes? Or both?" he asked.

"Pancakes?" Sarah asked, laughing. She looked at her watch. "It's after midnight!"

"I know, but we thought you might be hungry," Sam said. "Besides, it's always a good time for pancakes!"

Inside the hut, Doc was on the radio. He was talking to the station. He reported that they were all safe, and that the blizzard had blown through. He signed off, and smiled at Devin and Sarah as they sat down.

"Well, you two got a real taste of Antarctica," he said, as they sat down to eat. "You handled the situation perfectly. Good job!"

"The storm came in so fast," said Sarah. She poured syrup on her pancakes. "Good thing we had survival training," she added, smiling at Doc. Sam reached for another pancake. "It wasn't quite that exciting here," he said. "First the wind picked up. Then the sky suddenly turned dark, and it started to snow. By the time we reached the hut, we couldn't see more than a few feet in any direction."

Jean suddenly spoke up. "I guess you didn't pick up a signal from Lucky."

Devin and Sarah exchanged glances.

"No," Sarah said simply. "We tried before the storm hit and again just before we left."

Doc put down his fork. "I'm sorry. I know you were all fond of Lucky. Nature can seem cruel sometimes. But tomorrow, after you've all had a good night's sleep, maybe it won't seem so bad."

The interns all nodded. But no one spoke.

The next morning, they were back at work. With a receiver in hand, Sarah walked back and forth beside the corral. She was tracking three penguins at once that were out at sea.

Jean snapped a digital picture of Sarah at work. The interns still had a couple of weeks left at Cape Bird. But it wasn't too soon to start thinking about the final report they had to write for EcoAware. Jean had decided that morning that she needed more pictures of Doc and the others at work.

Jean turned toward the water. More pictures of penguins on ice floes would be good, too. She focused the camera on a big floe near shore. Several penguins were resting on it. Just as Jean was about to snap the picture, a familiar head broke the water's surface right in front of the floe.

"The leopard seal!" Jean shouted, pointing. "It's back."

Devin grabbed his binoculars to get a look at the predator. The seal was watching the penguins on the floe.

Devin panned the shoreline, looking for other penguins that might be in danger. One particular penguin caught his eye. It had just come out of the water. The sun glinted off something shiny on the penguin's back.

"Sarah," Devin said slowly. "Are any of our penguins out at sea right now?"

Sarah looked over at him. "Yes. Penguins 1, 4, and 19. But they're all pretty far right now."

"You're sure?" he asked.

"Yes, of course I'm sure," said Sarah, slightly irritated. "Why?"

"Because . . ." he said, pointing. "I think Lucky's back!"

Stunned, the interns and Doc watched as the little penguin hurried toward them.

"It *is* Lucky!" Sarah said gleefully. "He looks just fine!"

As Lucky waddled past Doc, the scientist began to chuckle.

"Well, there's the problem," he said, gesturing toward the penguin's back. "Lucky's transmitter is missing its antenna. That'll be easy to fix."

Lucky crossed the bridge and made his way to his nest. His mate, Number 6, seemed pleased to see him. The two birds touched their beaks and made soft clucking sounds.

"I wonder where he's been all this time," mused Sarah.

Doc stroked his beard. "I doubt if we'll ever know. A penguin faces a lot of dangers out there in the ocean. Leopard seals. Killer whales. The odd shark."

"Despite all that, Lucky survived," said Sam. "His name fits him pretty well."

A look of inspiration suddenly crossed Jean's face. She pulled out her notebook and started writing something.

"What's up, Jean?" Devin asked.

"I think I've got the lead for our report to EcoAware," she replied. "How about this:

'Penguins survive many dangers in Antarctica. But can they survive global warming?'"

"That's terrific, Jean," said Sam. Jean's face lit up with a smile.

"Well, then," said Doc, turning to look at the four of them. "If we're going to answer that puzzling scientific question, we'd better get back to work."

The EcoAware interns nodded in agreement. Suddenly, working here under the pale Antarctic sun, surrounded by fifty thousand penguins, seemed like the best job in the world.

Report to Dr. Bender

Imagine that Dr. Bender has asked you to write a one-page report about what you have learned about the environment and animals of Antarctica.

• Draw a cause-and-effect chart like the one below.

• Think about the causes and effects in the story. A cause is the reason something happens. An effect is the result, or what happens next.

• Look at the chart below for a sample.

• Fill in your chart with causes and effects that have to do with the environment and animals of Antarctica.

• Write a one-page report in which you explain two of the cause-and-effect relationships from your chart.

CAUSE	EFFECT
1. Global warming	1. The ice around Antarctica is melting faster.

Read More About Antarctica

Find and read more books about Antarctica. As you read, think about these questions. They will help you understand more about this topic.

- What is the climate of Antarctica?

- What types of wildlife are found in Antarctica?

- Why do scientists study Antarctica?

- What have scientists learned from their studies in Antarctica?

- How is Antarctica different from other continents?

SUGGESTED READING
Reading Expeditions
Scientists in the Field:
Protecting the Seas